CH00870656

CRYPTOCURRENCIES

How to Safely Create Stable and Long-term Passive Income by Investing in Cryptocurrencies

Table of Contents

INTRODUCTION

You're about to discover how to safely invest in cryptocurrencies potentially, earning you a secondary income in the most passive way possible.

The advent of technology has brought about a multitude of benefits for people across the world. These days, information is readily available, there are apps that make lifestyles more efficient, and there are different opportunities with which people can increase their income-generating capacities.

One such opportunity is via cryptocurrency investing. What you have here is a method of passive income generation; passive meaning that you do not really have to do a lot to earn money once you learn how the system works. Cryptocurrency investing, when done properly, can provide you with an excellent stream of passive income.

From this book, you will learn all about cryptocurrencies. You will gain insight on the different types of cryptocurrencies, trading exchanges, blockchains, and more. You will also learn about investing in these digital assets safely. There are risks that you have to be mindful of when it comes to these currencies and said risks are also mentioned in this book.

Hopefully, with the help of the contents of this book, you will gain enough confidence to try your hand at cryptocurrency investing.

Thank you and I hope you enjoy it!

CHAPTER 1

WHAT ARE CRYPTOCURRENCIES?

Many say that cryptocurrency will be the primary financial asset in the future. These days, there are plenty of individuals who are familiar with cryptocurrencies but there remain a significant number of people who are still clueless as to what these are and how they can benefit from them.

Aside from private individuals, government agencies, financial institutions, and numerous corporations few are well aware of what these are. These days, most of these agencies have actually invested in and continue to spend on cryptocurrency research. This just shows you how relevant these digital coins are in our modern society.

The thing about these digital financial assets is that not only have they sparked interest in people but they have also grown to become potential threats for others, especially banks. For the rest who are still confused about this trend, this is book was primarily written to explain what this new currencies are and how you can earn passive income by investing in them.

The Origin of Cryptocurrencies

Were you aware of the fact that cryptocurrencies came to light because someone was looking for a complementary product to digital funds? We have had digital cash reserves available on the Web for quite some time. Cryptocurrencies were made to serve as their side products.

The person who invented the first cryptocurrency, Bitcoin, was a man by the name of Satoshi Nakamoto. Regardless of how old Bitcoins are now, they remain to be some of the most valuable cryptocurrencies of recent times.

Before the concept of cryptocurrencies came about, digital cash was available via deposits made from debit cards and credit cards plus deposits to online payment channels made from physical bank accounts.

Digital cash during that time may have also referred to vouchers that could be purchased or provided as a marketing tactic. The problem with these though is that most of them were not designed well enough to prevent the onset of double spending.

The problem of double spending was what Bitcoins first addressed. These cryptocurrencies did not require any server, regulation, or authority. These relied on P2P networks as a means to ensure single spending. It is also to be noted that other attempts before Bitcoins failed miserably, thus, making Bitcoins truly revolutionary.

Aside from double spending, another issue that resulted in the creation of cryptocurrencies can be attributed to the failure of several third-party payment channels to provide a secure system that people can use to pay for things online.

Considering that these channels are highly-regulated, not to mention centralized in nature, and still they failed, Bitcoins were created to be independent of any central regulatory system and instead work on P2P trustworthiness as a foundation.

When it comes to digital cash, aside from worrying about transactions and balances, you also have to concern yourself with accounts, not to mention payment channels and methods. The problem with these payment channels is that they are highly susceptible to double spending.

Up until now, efforts are still being made to resolve this conundrum. But until servers are assessed, this problem will continue to exist as it is the balance-recording or monitoring agents that are responsible for the error.

The beauty of cryptocurrencies is that there is no server system that you need to worry about since they work with a decentralized network. With the P2P network at work, everyone has an updated list of transactions that they track, monitor, and check for problems.

Transactions occur between individuals and so there is a personal interest in the correctness of every transaction and record kept. This is why errors like double spending are eliminated. On most occasions, you can expect all participants to reach an absolute consensus on the legitimacy of trades.

The Basics of Cryptocurrencies

Here's an easy way to explain what cryptocurrencies are: a series of digital money that can be used to make purchases and similar transactions online. Just like traditional financial instruments, these can also be held as investments and traded when the right price surfaces.

Upon face value, cryptocurrencies are not actually digital coins per se but more of lines of code in a database. Changing these lines of code will not be easy as there are several conditions that need to be satisfied before any editing access is granted.

Weird as it may sound, the same concept applies to traditional currency, paper money and coinage. In this case, the database is your bank account and the money inside makes up the entries. There are specific conditions that need to be satisfied (identity verification) before you can access whatever is inside. Making changes pertain to deposits and withdrawals.

What Do Cryptocurrency Transactions Look Like?

There are seven steps involved in cryptocurrency transactions. Here they are:

1. A transaction is requested online. This can be a purchase, sale, or trade.

2. The request is sent to the P2P network. Instead of servers, the computer systems used here are referred to as nodes.

3. With the use of algorithms, the network then verifies the transaction and the requester's identity.

4. A transaction is verified and accepted or denied.

5. Approved or verified requests are logged on a digital database called a blockchain.

6. The new transaction is added to a pre-existing series of stored lines of code, which cannot be altered or erased.

7. The transaction is marked as complete.

Although cryptocurrency transactions may seem complex, these processes actually take a short amount of time to complete, some even within a minute or two. This is why cryptocurrency trades are seen as highly efficient and convenient compared to other traditional forms of currency.

When it comes to cryptocurrency transactions, you should be mindful of the fact that there are specific transactional properties that these possess. This means that even if there are no clear regulatory processes in play, there are still rules that apply to their purchase, sale, or trade.

Here are the main transactional properties that you should familiarize yourself with if you wish to invest in cryptocurrencies:

1. Transactions are anonymous.

Apart from this, accounts are anonymous as well. You might be thinking how this is possible when there are verification processes in place. Well, investors and traders have pseudonyms in the form of account links tied to their cryptocurrency accounts. For as long as the links are legitimate, your identity as a buyer or seller is deemed real.

2. All transactions cannot be reversed.

This means that once you have sent in payments for purchase or transferred coins as part of a sale, there is no way to gain either back if you change your mind. With transactions confirmed in minutes, you really have no safety net to work with. This is why it is always best to practice extreme caution before taking a decision

3.   Transactions are secure.

Although these are irreversible, all transactions are secure as cryptocurrencies are protected via cryptography. You need a special key to access your account. For as long as you have this key, you will not have to worry about your funds being taken without your knowledge.

4.   Cryptocurrencies are highly accessible.

You do not need to ask for any permission if you wish to buy or sell cryptocurrencies. All you have to do is download the necessary software online and you will gain access to these digital financial instruments.

5.   Transactions run globally.

Cryptocurrency transactions are coursed through computer networks and P2P systems. This means that transactions can be done through international markets with ease. All you need is a computer, a working connection to the Internet, and funds to invest in cryptocurrencies.

The Role of Cryptocurrency Miners

If you take a closer look at how cryptocurrency transactions work, you will notice that everything takes place within a network of peers and everyone in the system has access to transaction histories. This means that even if they cannot physically alter any database, they will be well aware of the balances of every single cryptocurrency account in the network.

In this case, you will have multiple entries that describe each transaction including who the participants are. The records will also contain confirmations of said transactions in the form of signatures that utilize the buyer or seller's private keys.

Once there is a new transaction, this is immediately inputted into the system and everyone on that peer-to-peer network will get wind of it. This is after all of the necessary confirmation processes have been completed. In the world of cryptocurrencies, verification and confirmation are the two main processes that identify legitimate transactions.

Without any confirmation, transactions remain as plain requests and at this stage, they can still be forged or cancelled. Upon confirmation, the transaction becomes irreversible and is added to the blockchain. Cryptocurrency miners are in charge of creating the different coins and also confirming all relevant transactions in the P2P network.

Only these miners have the right to confirm cryptocurrency transactions. What they do is take all the requests and run the various verification processes. They then determine which requests are legitimate and which are to be voided. Legitimate requests are approved, stamped, confirmed, and added to the blockchain. All confirmed transactions must be added to the blockchain by all computers in the network.

Cryptocurrency miners perform the most important task in the entire chain but they are not paid in paper money or coinage. What they get are tokens and cryptocurrencies that they can use for various online exchanges. The great thing about this setup is that anyone can become a cryptocurrency miner.

Keep in mind that there is no official regulating body in place. There is only a P2P network. Although anyone can mine coins, there are protocols in place to ensure that no one monopolizes or takes advantage of the trade. This is where specialized mechanisms enter the picture. These mechanisms work by preventing fraudulent or abusive transactions from occurring.

The founder of Bitcoins, Satoshi Nakamoto, created a rule for those who want to be coin miners. First, they are obligated to invest in a special computer to be worthy of the role. Their computer system must be able to accommodate special functions (large chunks of data are converted into more manageable links).

Also, they must make an effort to find a new hash that is compatible with the previous one used in the blockchain. If they fail to do this, it will not be possible for them to connect any new block within the existing chain. In simpler terms, they need to solve a puzzle that will enable them to build blocks and add these to the blockchain. For Satoshi Nakamoto, this proof of work and capacity is essential to ensure the continuous protection or security of cryptocurrencies.

When a miner is able to add blocks to the blockchain, he will then garner a certain amount of coins. The more blocks he is able to add to the network, the more coins he earns, hence the term cryptocurrency mining. The catch is that the hardware and software investments can be rather steep and you can only mine a certain number of coins per attempt.

Are cryptocurrencies real currencies?

Cryptocurrencies hold real value and they are purchased with real money but they work more like stocks rather than the bills and coins we use today. They are stocks in technology but can be traded for other cryptocurrencies not to mention real-world currencies.

These days, there are certain types like Bitcoin, for example, that can be used to make product purchases and service payments both online and offline. So in this sense, you can consider them as real currencies as they have this certain usability. What you should note though is that there are types that are more liquid than others but not as liquid as real-world money.

CHAPTER 2

THE DIFFERENT TYPES OF CRYPTOCURRENCIES

With cryptocurrencies, you have digital financial instruments that can eventually replace paper money and coinage. These days, more facilities are accepting this mode of payment for products and services. But do know that there are hundreds of different cryptocurrencies, all of which have been birthed by the concept of Bitcoins.

There really is no need to go through every single one of these cryptocurrencies. In this book, our focus will be on the top ten, the most widely used cryptocurrency types that you should consider investing in.

1. Bitcoin

As mentioned previously, Bitcoin is the first form of cryptocurrency ever created. You can use these to make product purchases and pay for services online and offline. These are also becoming easier to purchase with Bitcoin ATMs being launched in different countries.

The beauty of Bitcoins is that you can buy or sell them even if you are not all too familiar with how they work. You do not need to understand the technical side of things to benefit from these coins. They are known for being very beginner friendly.

2. Ether

Unlike traditional coins, there are smart contracts tied to Ether. This is why this form of cryptocurrency offers more protection not only for buyers, but sellers as well. Trading coins even with people that you do not know of will not entail a high level of risk. You can use Ether to pay for things as well.

3. Litecoin

This type of cryptocurrency closely resembles Bitcoin with the only difference being that transactions are run using an open-source protocol.

4. Chinacoin

Developed as a form of Litecoin, Chinacoin offers an additional layer of security by using script-based keys. This means that private keys are not that easy to access offering the owner more protection for his coins.

5. Ripple

When it comes to Ripple, you have the type of cryptocurrency that is processed in the same way as the standard paper money and coins. Distribution relies on a consensus, there are formal exchange protocols executed per transaction, and everything is coded on a ledger.

6. Peercoin

Those who are rather patient will find this particular cryptocurrency appealing. Peercoins work pretty much like Bitcoins but they are not as easy to mine the first time around. But the more you persist in mining them, the easier the hashing process becomes.

7. Primecoin

Most cryptocurrencies have been developed using the Bitcoin system but Primecoin begs to differ. It has been created using a hash system based on prime numbers hence the name. By using prime numbers, it is possible to create coins that can easily be mined but are more secure to hold.

8. Dogecoin

Most people refer to the Dogecoin as enhanced Bitcoin. Unlike other cryptocurrencies, there is no limit as to how much of these coins can be mined. The catch is that they carry a far smaller value compared to the other types of coins. But this is a good thing if you are someone who often engages in small transactions offline and online.

9. Dash

Think of Dash as Bitcoin's introvert-ish sibling. People who want to invest in a more secretive form of cryptocurrency will appreciate the higher level of anonymity that Dash offers. All relevant transactions are coursed through a special network where transactions are untraceable.

10. Ven

Ven was developed for a particular group, Hub Culture, but has since become a publicly tradable form of cryptocurrency. What sets it apart from other digital coins is that it actively makes an effort to counteract inflation. This means that the value of the coins is not highly susceptible to rapid increases or drops.

If you are new to cryptocurrencies then it is suggested that you start investing in Bitcoins. As you gain experience in the market, that is when you should try other forms of cryptocurrency. By no means should you expect them to perform in the same manner as they have their own patrons that dictate movements and trends.

CHAPTER 3

HOW TO PURCHASE CRYPTOCURRENCIES

Cryptocurrencies are digital assets that are gaining more international popularity as time progresses. These can be mined, bought, and traded over dedicated exchange platforms. There are also a number of different applications that can be used to conduct direct trades not to mention find cryptocurrency buyers and sellers all over the map.

For those who are interested in investing in these cryptocurrencies, one of the first things to think about is converting money into these digital currencies. The easiest way to do this is through a simple purchase transaction.

1. Buy cryptocurrencies via exchange platforms.

Again, there are exchanges where these currencies can be traded in. Most of these exchange platforms also offer a variety of cryptocurrencies for sale. Keep in mind though that these currencies are in no way owned by the exchangers. Think of the latter as a commercial bank that stores, trades, and offers money to the public.

When you utilize an exchange, not only can you convert real money into cryptocurrencies but you can also convert them back when needed. It is also possible to use a particular cryptocurrency to purchase one of the other varieties. Considering the variety of services that you can avail of from an exchange, finding the one suitable to your needs is truly essential.

When choosing an exchange, the decision does not only boil down the transaction fees they charge or how many payment channels they can accommodate. There are certain exchanges that only accommodate a particular category of cryptocurrencies so you really want to have a clear decision as to what particular cryptocurrency you wish to invest in early on.

The most commonly traded cryptocurrency today is Bitcoin so if you are new to these digital currencies, it would be a safe bet to start with them. If you find your interest in those which have only been released recently, you might find it quite challenging to locate an exchange that has already updated its system to accommodate these. Not to say that there are no exchanges available. It is just that you have to be ready to spend more time during your search for exchanges.

Apart from this, do know that Bitcoins can be traded for a number of real-world currencies while other types of digital currencies may only be traded with Bitcoins. So it is also necessary that you be mindful of the different trading pairs that are being offered by your shortlisted exchanges.

Although it was mentioned earlier that service fees need not be the basis of your decision when it comes to selecting an exchange, it is still relevant in this entire process. Most of the time, beginners only consider the trade or transaction fees; these pertains to the percentage that the exchange earns per transaction. This fee can vary from one exchange to another. You will find some that charge small fees while others may be entitled to as much as 5% of your total earnings.

Aside from the trade fees, there are also standard usage fees (fixed monthly service fees) as well as deposit and withdrawal charges that you need to pay close attention to. Most of the time, the highest miscellaneous charge will come from withdrawals as the exchange transfers real money into your chosen channel. This is why it is important to find an exchange that has close ties with local financial institutions in your area as this ensures lower transfer fees.

Exchanges are not heavily regulated and this is a fact that you should never forget. There are those which have been able to stand the tests of time and continue to provide valuable services to cryptocurrency investors while there are some which have closed down for good. In the case of the latter, there have been reports of unfulfilled payments and this is why you need to do extensive research.

Aside from the exchanges' reputation, you also have to take a look at their security protocols. All of this information should be readily available online or in their websites. If you cannot find enough information about a particular exchange, that is your signal to start looking for a completely different platform.

2. Buy cryptocurrencies via a cryptocurrency wallet.

A part of the cryptocurrency investment process involves the usage of a cryptocurrency wallet. There are exchanges that offer this added feature while others will require you to visit a third-party provider for your storage needs.

You will find that there are a number of these storage facilities that also offer direct buying and selling of cryptocurrencies. Unlike exchanges where the rates vary from seller to seller, with cryptocurrency wallets there usually is a fixed rate that applies for both purchasing and dispensing. All you have to do to make a purchase is to link your credit card or bank account information to your cryptocurrency wallet.

Upon first glance, it seems as if this option of purchasing cryptocurrencies is the best one to consider. But before you make any final decision on the matter, know that just like other methods available, purchasing coins through your digital wallet also has its fair share of pros and cons.

Let's start with why it is good to consider:

- Transactions are quick to accomplish here. You can compare it to any online shopping site where you choose a product, add it to your card, enter your payment details, and that is about it.

- Identity verification is a breeze as you simply have to link your payment information to the system to start making purchases.

- You can find ATMs that now cater to cryptocurrencies so you can directly buy coins there. Kiosks are also being developed for the same purpose and there is also an ongoing initiative to start offering cryptocurrencies in retail establishments like convenience stores and agencies such as post offices.

But it also has several points of concern:

- Transactions may be fast but there are limitations as to the trading pairs being offered by cryptocurrency wallets. This means that there may be real-world currencies that they will not accept.

- Your privacy may be at risk when you connect your personal information and payment details in the system. Cryptocurrencies are founded on the concept of trader anonymity but this is defeated by having transactions tied to your identity.

3. Buy cryptocurrencies via P2P

Cryptocurrencies can also be bought via peer-to-peer transactions. If you have a friend who owns coins that you want then you can ask them to sell and vice versa. The important thing here is finding a seller who is willing to part with their coins. There are exchanges that work simply by connecting buyers and sellers around the world so this is a good option to consider. There are also communities and forums that you can participate in if you wish to find these people by yourself.

Aside from your personal network and those from exchanges, you can also work with your wallet provider as some have local trading tools built into the system. Here, you will be connected to sellers within your area and you will be able to converse with them directly. If you make a purchase or vice versa, the transaction will immediately be reflected into your wallet.

You might be thinking how safe such transactions can be. Well, you can always use online tools, investor testimonials, and such to check the legitimacy of the seller. If you will be working on a platform for this, you will benefit from the ratings that each account holder has. But the decision will always be yours to make and the consequences yours to bear. So be careful and smart so that you find a trustworthy individual to work with.

Here are a couple more things that you should bear in mind when buying cryptocurrencies via P2P. If transactions are not to be done digitally, make sure that you transact in a public place. Meeting someone for the first time, for such a transaction can be scary and having tons of other people around will help safeguard you from the cons.

Online, be careful as there are phishing sites everywhere. Always go the extra mile and verify not only the individual's identity but the platform that you will be using for the transaction. This will ensure that your personal and financial information will be safe from prying eyes. Also be careful when it comes to phishing emails and such.

4. Buy cryptocurrencies via credit card.

These days, thanks to the evolution of online payment channels and systems, you can also buy your chosen cryptocurrencies using your credit card. But do remember that just like with other things that you can purchase online, there still remain several risks when you charge purchases to your credit card.

The great thing about credit cards is that most of them, especially Visa and MasterCard, are accepted by all platforms and payments can be accommodated regardless of what home currency it is that you are using. This is because any monetary conversion can be accommodated by your home bank.

5. Buy cryptocurrencies via wire.

You will find some individuals or exchanges for that matter that accept wire transfers as modes of payment. The problem though is that these transfers can take days to complete.

6. Buy cryptocurrencies via online payment channels.

Online payment channels like PayPal, for example, can also be used to purchase cryptocurrencies. You have the option of linking your credit card to the system or using your internal wallet for the transaction. Do expect additional service fees here but do know that these fees actually protect you as these systems almost always come with dispute protocols wherein failed transactions or complaints will merit an investigation and may lead to your money being returned to your account.

7. Buy cryptocurrencies via cash.

Especially for P2P arrangements, you can also use cash to purchase your chosen coins. In this case, you can choose to pay cash outright during a meet-up or use cash funds in a digital wallet during your transaction. Either way it is the quickest mode of payment available today, online or offline.

So there you have it. There are plenty of different ways by which you can purchase cryptocurrencies to start your investment journey with. Just make sure that you do your research before choosing a particular option. It will also be wise to try several methods out then determine which one works best in your favor.

CHAPTER 4

CRYPTOCURRENCY INVESTMENT

If you've read up to this point, it is safe to assume that you have developed an interest in cryptocurrencies. But before you make any initial investment, here are some things to familiarize yourself with.

Cryptocurrencies function more as stocks rather than fiat currency, traditional paper and coinage. The minute you buy your first cryptocurrency, this means that you are purchasing a stock in technology. It can be one block of a blockchain or an even larger chunk of the cryptocurrency network.

1. Budget

The first step to investing in cryptocurrencies is actually having the budget for it. All transactions involve starting capital so you need to check the prices out. This will help you figure out just how much fiat currency you need to start your investment journey.

2. Cryptocurrency Type

The next step is to decide on which particular cryptocurrency you want to invest in. There are hundreds available today. As a beginner, you will be safer by delving in those that are rather common like Bitcoins or Ether, for example.

You can find summaries of the top coins in this book but do know that you can also consult other resources for this information. It is always best to do ample research when it comes to something like this. Check out the pros and cons, accessibility, value, and of course, tradability.

3. Exchange

When you have decided on a particular type of cryptocurrency, now is the time to find yourself an exchange. The exchange will serve as your transaction platform. Here, you can buy, sell, and actively trade an assortment of coins for fiat currency or coins for coins, depending on your preference.

Note that exchanges differ in terms of their offerings and the types of cryptocurrencies that they can accommodate so again, do your research before creating an account. Also check for payment methods at this point as not all exchanges accommodate all available payment channels.

4. Wallet

If your chosen exchange does not provide any access to cryptocurrency storage, find yourself a wallet to safekeep your coins. There are several kinds of wallets that can be chosen from.

5. Insurance

When it comes to cryptocurrencies, insurance is good to have. There are exchanges that offer this added service while others do not. In the case of the latter, you can work with third-party providers but doing so may entail additional costs.

6. Buying and Selling

You need to have coins to be able to participate in the market. Aside from your exchange, you can also buy coins from other people or websites. When you are working with other people, you simply need to provide them with your public key so that they can transfer the cryptocurrencies to your account.

On your part, you can work out the payment scheme directly. Usually, it involves a bank transfer. Once the transfer has been completed, you can expect to see your account's stocks increase. Everything is logged into a digital ledger for easy tracking.

7. Trading

If you want to trade your coins for another type of cryptocurrency, all you have to do is check your exchange for any available trading pair. In some cases, you can also trade your coins for fiat currencies other than your home currency. Common available currencies include USD and British Pounds.

With cryptocurrencies, you are limited to other coin types and fiat currencies when it comes to trading. You cannot use your coins to trade for commodities and metals like gold or silver.

Questions to Ask

When it comes to cryptocurrency investments, you will be dealing with non-concrete assets. This is why there are several questions that you need to answer prior to making any purchase or trade.

- Can I trust the developer?

When you invest in something, you should be able to preserve your capital and generate earnings from it. So can you trust the coin developer to provide you with something like this? Is your supplier credible enough to be allowed to hold onto your money?

- How valuable is my chosen cryptocurrency?

There are different types of cryptocurrencies, some of which are more valuable and popular than others. You have to be certain that your coin of choice will not lose its value or relevance overnight. This is why research matters.

- How long should I participate in the market?

You can choose to participate in the cryptocurrency market for as long as you like. As there are no heavily-binding contracts involved, you can always exit when you find the need to. In this case, what you need to do is prepare several strategies.

Focus on three things here:

1. Consider a bullish market.

2. Consider a bearish market.

3. Consider a break-even market.

Trading Strategies to Consider

You can start with these simple strategies as you engage in the cryptocurrency trade:

1. Arbitrage

Here, transactions are relatively quick. You will be able to earn a profit by buying low and selling high. For this to be possible, you can try buying coins from one exchange and selling it on another. There are no prevailing market rates when it comes to cryptocurrencies, so being observant goes a long way.

Arbitrage is all about exploiting available opportunities. But what you have to be careful of are the transaction fees charged by the exchanges as these can eat up your profits.

2. Short-Term Trading

This is all about leveraged trading. Case in point, you purchase a cryptocurrency that is currently moving upward in price. You then hold it for a few hours up to a few days then trade it off once the sale price becomes higher than the amount you paid for.

Here, you need to engage in frequent trades to earn a sizeable income but the beauty of short-term trading is that you are almost always assured of a margin per transaction.

CHAPTER 5

CRYPTOCURRENCY CHARACTERISTICS

Cryptocurrencies have three distinct characteristics:

1. They bear no physical form, only existing digitally.

2. There is no central body that regulates cryptocurrencies, states their value, or influences supply and demand.

3. Cryptocurrencies do not carry any intrinsic value and therefore cannot be traded with commodities like gold and other precious metals. It can only be traded with paper currencies.

It is also important to note that although cryptocurrencies are not officially regulated by financial or government agencies, the supply of coins remains to be controlled, usually by those who issue the different currencies. As a result, calculating the available supply at any given moment is simple to do. There is no guessing game involved in the process.

The beauty of cryptocurrencies is that they function as IOUs. Due to the informal nature of IOUs, they cannot and will never be classified as debts for those who invest in them. Cryptocurrencies are comparable to actual currencies, paper money and coinage, for example, but only have usable values in a different environment, which is the digital space.

CHAPTER 6

CRYPTOCURRENCY EXCHANGES

Before you start investing in cryptocurrencies, it would be wise to understand how exchanges work and what particular platforms you can work with.

Cryptocurrency Exchanges: What are They Really?

As cryptocurrencies are digital currencies, the exchanges where they are traded in are digital platforms, websites, which offer transactions like buying, selling, or trading. A cryptocurrency exchange works pretty much like a traditional stock or Forex exchange system. Professional brokers are accessible, self-trading is possible, and there are tools available to help you maximize each transaction.

Since transactions are coursed on the Web, these exchange platforms need to verify the identities of their participants. Just like social media accounts, email accounts, and such, you also need to create a user account in your platform of choice. You will then have to verify this account by providing the site with a valid identification card.

Although most exchanges require that participants have verified accounts, you will find others that are not too strict. The commonality between these exchanges is that they can accommodate self-made, straightforward trades.

The Different Kinds of Cryptocurrency Exchanges

There are different kinds of cryptocurrencies and there are also varying exchanges available to those who have investments or want to trade these digital assets. To start you off, here are the three primary exchanges that you can consider if you want to take part in the world of cryptocurrencies.

1. Brokers

What you have with brokers are websites that exist for the sole purpose of selling cryptocurrencies. It is the broker site that sets the price. A cryptocurrency broker is comparable to an outlet that offers foreign exchange services.

2. Trading Platforms

The trading platforms for cryptocurrencies work by connecting buyers and sellers in one place. The sites earn their income by taking a certain percentage off from every transaction done in the portal. You can say that this is their service fee. Trading platforms are excellent channels for simple, straightforward trading.

3. Direct Trading Systems

Direct trading systems are different from your everyday cryptocurrency trading platforms because they can accommodate more complex trades within the platform. Aside from just being a place for buying or selling cryptocurrencies, participants can actually engage in dynamic exchanges within the system.

In addition, the platform does not only offer buying or selling but constant trading amongst investors around the world. Unlike standard platforms, traders are not bound by set market prices for their cryptocurrencies. They can actually set their own prices for these digital assets. It is now in the discretion of the other investors if they want to proceed with an exchange or not.

As you can see, the types of exchanges for cryptocurrency vary from basic to complex. As an investor, you can expect yourself to go through all of these channels as you engage in the trade.

What Should You Look for in a Cryptocurrency Exchange?

Just like with other investment channels, it is important that you do not simply go with the first option that you see. In this case, you will be dealing with digital assets that carry real monetary values. This is why you should not leave anything to chance. Before you even consider buying cryptocurrencies to trade with, you should do some research as there are different exchanges available online.

If you do not know where to begin, here are some guidelines that may hopefully help in your search for the most suitable exchange.

- Credibility

Credibility is essential when it comes to cryptocurrency trading. You do not want to lose your investment or experience unnecessary problems just because you did not check your chosen exchange out.

You have the Internet on your side, use it to your benefit. Aside from checking the platform itself, search for relevant reviews from people who have actually used the platform with success. Asking for referrals is another excellent option. Also, there are trustworthy industry websites that can be consulted as well. If you need more assistance, you can even participate in forums.

• Registration Process and Requirements

Simplicity is the name of the game when it comes to account creation. You want to create a trading account in a few minutes and successfully verify it in an equally short amount of time. Especially since you are working in the digital space, your chosen exchange should be optimized enough to have an efficient integrated registration system.

If your exchange cannot even perfect the registration process, just think of how problematic the platform may be when it comes to the actual transaction interface. Having practical verification processes is also important. Most of the time, exchanges that are not able to quickly verify accounts do not have the right technology for that purpose. In this case, chances are they will not also have the right technologies for the service or security.

- Verification and Security

Although verification is important, it should not be excessive or unrealistic in terms of identification requirements. Usually, a government-issued ID card will be enough to allow you to deposit or withdraw money from your account. Verification may take anywhere from a few minutes to several days but it ensures that your account and transactions are always secure.

You will find exchanges that will permit you to transact in the system anonymously. These are the exchanges that you should watch out for. Usually, they offer minimal security or encryption that can easily jeopardize your transactions, not to mention your trading account on the platform. It would be best if you went through with the whole verification process for something like this. Protect yourself from hackers and scams.

- Geographical Conditions or Restrictions

Just like how Forex trading is regulated, the same applies to cryptocurrencies. As a result, site functionalities may differ from one location to another. There may be some tools that you can access in one country and not in another. This is why you should find an exchange that is fully-compatible given your country's geographical regulations.

- Exchange Rates

When it comes to exchange rates, these actually differ from one platform to another. This is why you should practice the concept of "shopping around" when you search for cryptocurrency exchanges. There are times when an exchange would have rates that are significantly lower than the market rate. You may also be lucky enough to find high exchange rates that will work in your favor. So spend time comparing rates and services so that you can land with the best deal on a secure exchange platform.

- Transaction and Service Fees

What you have here are pieces of information that should not be kept hidden by exchanges. It is necessary for them to publish these service and transaction rates in the site and you should definitely look for them when you pay the page a visit.

These fees tend to differ depending on the exchange. They are usually dependent on the extent of services that your membership comes with. If you are in a simple buying and selling exchange platform, you can expect lower rates compared to those that offer consistent trading.

In this case, the concept of "better service higher rates" does not always apply. This is why you should not base your decision simply on this component. What you have to set your mind to is finding a credible exchange that meets your needs and offers its services at a reasonable rate.

• Payment Methods and Processes

Keep in mind that cryptocurrencies involve real money. This is why you need to think about how you can pay and get paid should you decide to invest in these digital assets. When you assess potential exchanges to consider, find information with regard to the payment methods as well.

There are exchanges that offer credit or debit card transactions. Some may involve direct bank deposits. You will find others that patronize wire transfers while there are others that are more efficient as they leverage digital payment services like PayPal.

It is important that you find an exchange that can accommodate as many payment options as possible. Remember that you will be transacting with other people on the platform and you never know which method it is that they have access to. The more payment methods are accommodated by the platform, the more convenient it will be for you to transact in that system.

Aside from convenience, payment options also dictate transaction speeds. For example, credit card transactions are secure yet easier to verify and because of this, transactions are processed in minutes. As for wire transfers on the other hand, these require manual processing by banks and may take several days, sometimes even weeks to complete.

Cryptocurrency Exchanges to Consider

As cryptocurrencies rose in popularity over the years, plenty of exchanges have popped up online. This makes it even more challenging, especially for beginners, to find the right platform to start with. To assist you in your search, here are some of the best exchanges that are worth your consideration.

It is suggested that you start with these so that you can easily get the hang of cryptocurrency investing. Here you have exchanges that actual users have rated to be top notch. You will also find those which have been rated based on their accessibility and functionality. And then there are those that trump the rest when it comes to security and transaction fees.

1. Gemini

It is primarily serving the purpose of trading Ether and Bitcoin cryptocurrencies. It is a highly-secure exchange platform. It offers a user-friendly interface and has regulated standards not to mention capital requirements. It functions closely like an actual bank and is highly liquid ensuring that you will get paid. Here, you can trade both cryptocurrency types with US dollars and vice versa.

2. Coinbase

Millions of traders are currently using Coinbase, making it one of the most popular exchanges available today. Aside from beginners, well-known traders are also taking part in the cryptocurrency game through this platform. The edge of Coinbase is that it offers a wide variety of tools and services yet is user-friendly. The transactions are secured and it even offers a built-in storage for your cryptocurrencies.

3. Bitstamp

With Bitstamp, you have one of the earliest trading platforms made available for Bitcoin. User-friendly yet highly-secure, it also offers Bitcoin storage within the platform. The best thing about the latter is that all stored Bitcoins are insured. User support is available all day every day. You can create a free account and begin participating in the trade. It is very easy and efficient to use.

4. Cexio

With Cexio, you have a universal cryptocurrency exchange platform. You can easily conduct trades here exchanging actual money for cryptocurrencies and vice versa. It is ideal for both newbies and experienced traders. Armed with user-friendly tools and functions, it is a great platform to start with. Also, the advantage you gain by using Cexio is with regard to its prices which closely reflect those of the markets.

5. Poloniex

Security is extremely important in the cryptocurrency game and this is something that can be expected from Poloniex, as an exchange platform. It supports hundreds of different cryptocurrencies and trading pairs, and offers a series of tools both for novices and advanced investors alike. The beauty of this platform is that you can always expect to close a position.

6. Kraken

If your chosen cryptocurrency is the Bitcoin, then Kraken would be an ideal exchange option. It is one of the largest Bitcoin trading platforms available today. It is even a partner of the primary digital bank for cryptocurrencies. Although it is mainly used to trade Bitcoins, it can also accommodate Ether transactions and those involving other cryptocurrencies. It is the exchange of choice for traders who have more experience in the industry.

7. Shapeshift

As what was previously mentioned, there are certain exchanges that allow for anonymous trades. In this case, you can easily make straightforward trades without registering for an account with the help of Shapeshift. This will be an ideal exchange to use if you plan on making transactions using nothing else but cryptocurrencies.

CHAPTER 7

STORING CRYPTOCURRENCIES

Cryptocurrencies are digital assets and because they function much like actual money you need a place to store your coins in. With ordinary money, you have safes, wallets, banks, and the like. Although there are storage facilities available for cryptocurrencies, these are more complex compared to traditional wallets.

Cryptocurrency transactions are recorded in a blockchain. On this blockchain are wallets that are made available to account holders. You will also find wallets being offered by exchange platforms and other third-party service providers.

But the wallet for cryptocurrencies is not comparable to a storage box, for example. In this case, you are working with a URL that is linked to the blockchain. This is an exclusive link. When you visit it, you will be directed to a page on the blockchain website. This is why you need to be connected to the Internet if you wish to access your cryptocurrency wallet.

If you invest in cryptocurrencies, you will have a wallet with two addresses, one of which is a public one and the other private. You need the public address so that other people can send you money or coins when you engage in buying or selling transactions. As for the private one, it is protected by a password and will provide you access to the funds should you wish to make a deposit or withdrawal. You also use the private account to send funds to other cryptocurrency holders.

What you have to do in this case is keep your private key safe. Unless you need to spend any of your available funds, never reveal this key to anyone as it will give them full access to your money. These are the basics that you should know when it comes to cryptocurrency storage.

You can use different types of wallets if you have cryptocurrencies to store. There are five main kinds of wallets that you can choose from.

1. Paper

You might be wondering how paper can be used to store digital currencies. Well, in this case, the paper wallet serves to store your cryptocurrency keys. Basically, you write the keys down and put the paper in a safe place.

2. Mobile

There are mobile apps that serve the purpose of helping you manage your cryptocurrencies. These mobile wallets are excellent options for those who regularly utilize their cryptocurrencies. The safety issue here is hacking. And if you just so happen to lose your phone, you will also be in a big trouble.

3. Online

What you have here is the simplest wallet to have and the easiest one to use. The problem is that it is not as secure as other available options. This is ideal for short-term storage. So if you are looking for a place to store funds for regular purchases or trades, this is something worth considering.

4. Desktop

This is similar to the mobile app. The only difference is that the app needs to be installed in your desktop computer.

5. Hardware Device

This is a device that has been created for the sole purpose of storing keys for cryptocurrency accounts. You can say that this is the most secure option available but still have susceptibilities especially to external factors that can damage gadgets; like spilled water, for example.

Cryptocurrencies are currently in a bullish market and this means that prices may be expected to soar without warning. When this happens, more people, hackers most specially, will find interest in cryptocurrencies. This is why you should protect your coins by all means possible. You do not want them falling into the wrong hands.

With this in mind, do consider making an investment in your cryptocurrency wallet as well; apart from your investment in the coins themselves. Do not settle on whatever is provided free of charge. Think about features like convenience, accessibility, and most importantly, security.

There are different characteristics that your cryptocurrency wallet must possess. Especially if you are new to these digital coin keepers, you can use these as guidelines to help narrow down your options.

- Convenience

When choosing a cryptocurrency wallet, see to it that you find something that will enable you to use your coins whenever you need to. This may be during a point of sale or at the point of purchase. Basically, you want something that is compatible with different coins, software, and exchange platforms.

- Accessibility

Accessibility is also important. Being able to use your coins when needed is a must. If you cannot get a hold of your cryptocurrencies then what is the purpose of investing in them in the first place? Access in this sense should be 24/7.

- Security

It is crucial that you do your research when it comes to how well a particular provider secures their coins. In this case, check the track record of the storage provider. Check if they have had cases of tampering or hacking. It will also be a good idea if you looked for testimonials with regard to their security protocols.

- Utility

User-friendliness is essential when it comes to something like this. If you do not know how to use the digital wallet then you will not gain easy access to your coins. Also, if you cannot utilize the different functions available, you might end up leaving your coins unsecured on a digital platform.

- Cost

How much of a budget do you have for cryptocurrency storage? The cost of the wallet itself is important. With free wallets, you will be entitled to basic functions. So if you need something that is more complex or secure for that matter, be prepared to spend a little extra money.

These days, there are several wallets available for investors to use and here are some that are worth your consideration. What you should remember though is that every option has its fair share of advantages and cons so spend time doing ample research. If you need to test several of these out, go right ahead. Doing so will help you find the most suitable cryptocurrency wallet for your specific needs.

1. Online Wallet

   • Coinbase

   Online, you also have a great option in terms of cryptocurrency wallets and it is called Coinbase. Actually, what you have here is also referred to as a hot wallet as it functions together with an exchange platform. Here, not only can you store your coins but also engage in active trades instantaneously; doing so is free of charge too.

   Unlike other wallets, your coins have full insurance here. All you need is to undergo a two-step verification process to set things up. You can even choose to increase your wallet's security by enabling Google's authenticator function. On the exchange, you also have the opportunity to up your security even more as Coinbase also offers vault storage.

If there is a downside to this particular wallet, it is that it is not compatible with other types of cryptocurrency. You can only use it to store your Bitcoins and Ethereum coins.

2. Paper Wallet

• My Ether Wallet

Paper wallets are also rather popular amongst the cryptocurrency market participants. Those who want something simple yet gets the job done will love this option. For one, it does not call for a significant monetary investment. Hardware wallets, for example, can cost a pretty penny. Instead of paying for a wallet, these people may prefer to spend the cash to purchase more coins.

Online, there is a paper wallet website called My Ether Wallet. When you visit the site, you can create a wallet carrying your cryptocurrency keys. Unlike other unsecured sites, this one will not transmit or store any private information that you provide. If you still feel uneasy about revealing your private keys, you have the option of downloading the standalone program, which you can then use offline.

The thing about paper wallets is that they are quick to generate and free to use. They are more ideal for those who have been using cryptocurrency wallets for some time. This is because setting them up is what takes time and requires experience. Because of this, newbies might not find them simple to utilize.

3. Hardware Device Wallet

- KeepKey

Much like an external hard drive albeit smaller, you can expect a cool and unique tech gadget when you avail of what is known as KeepKey. If you do not mind a little bit of weight then this is a strong safeguard for your coins.

Be careful though that given its weight, it can be more prone to being damaged when dropped compared to other, much lighter alternatives.

This is ideal for those who are interested in something reliable yet simple to use. Even non-tech individuals will not have issues with the user-friendly interface that KeepKey comes with.

- Trezor

One of the first wallets of this type includes Trezor. If you are interested in something offering maximum encryption and security then this is the ideal option to consider for your cryptocurrencies. Aside from physical thievery, you also get virtual safeguarding for your coins.

If there is a downside to this wallet, and if things like aesthetics concern you, then you might not like its substandard looks. But if style is a non-issue then you will highly benefit from the security that Trezor can provide you with. Many consider this to be vault-like because it is even capable of protecting your cryptocurrencies from malware attacks.

- Nano Ledger S

What sets the Nano Ledger S apart from other hardware storage systems is that it is one of the most reliable, though highly affordable models available today. It is smaller in size compared to other hardware wallets not to mention lighter making it extremely portable. If what you want is something easy to use and handy to carry around, then this might be the option to consider.

4. Software Wallet

- Electrum

When it comes to software wallets, let us start with the one called Electrum. What you have here is lightweight and is quick to access. Aside from being desktop-ready, you can also use it in your favorite mobile devices. What most users love about Electrum is that the developers were quite generous when it came to the wallet's features.

Aside from having the ability to accommodate a wide variety of cryptocurrencies, this particular wallet can also provide users with hardware wallet integration, anonymous access, cold storage, and a high level of security. And even if it is a type of software, it is not susceptible to downtime as it makes no use of any server system.

- Jaxx

Another type of software wallet that needs your attention goes by the name of Jaxx. The name alone can make you curious as to what it can provide you with. Jaxx is the first mobile-ready cryptocurrency wallet. It is able to accommodate a multitude of devices not to mention varying operating systems from iOS to Android.

These days, the software has been upgraded to work just as well with desktop systems making it all the more appealing. If you need to have your wallet across multiple devices, backups and transfers are a breeze with Jaxx. It functions much like an app where you can scan QR codes, send out and receive coins, and view a transaction log.

But given its different features, a more complex interface can be expected. This means that new users and non-tech people might encounter several challenges as they try to manipulate the app. The learning curve is rather steep but if you have the patience and the time needed to learn the ropes then you will end up with a great cryptocurrency wallet.

CHAPTER 8

TRACKING CRYPTOCURRENCIES

If you plan on investing in cryptocurrencies, then you need to track coins and their prices. Surely you will eventually invest in more than one kind of coin so it is best to have the right tools on hand.

The thing about cryptocurrencies is that just like other financial instruments, they can still be susceptible to volatility. This means that price shifts will never be absent from the equation.

If you take a closer look at these digital currencies, you will realize that it is the absence of regulation that actually causes this volatility threat. As coin owners dictate their own prices based on what buyers are willing to pay for coins, they can easily influence the movement of the market.

As a result, uncertainty will always be something you need to watch out for. In this case, uncertainty does not only cover prices and supply but coin value as well. Considering that there are hundreds of different cryptocurrencies available for trading, you never know which one will suddenly lose patrons and fall out of the market completely.

There are different apps online that you can use to track cryptocurrencies. Some only cater to Bitcoins or Ether while others accommodate other types of coins. What these apps do is track the prices relative to fiat currencies.

Here are some of the cryptocurrency trackers that you should consider especially if you are new to the entire investment thing.

1.   BitcoinWisdom

In the world of cryptocurrencies, Bitcoins are not only the first type ever created but continues to exist as the most popular one in the market. This being said, there are numerous exchanges that primarily accommodate them. The same can be said for price trackers.

BitcoinWisdom is a price tracker that works with Bitcoins as the base. What it does is track the price of Bitcoins in relation to fiat currencies and other coins. The great thing about this is that it provides real-time updates. As the user, you can control graphical information by setting time intervals. You can choose a timestamp of one second to one week.

2. Coinbase

Coinbase does not only help cryptocurrency investors track relevant price movements. It also offers other related investment features. But when it comes to the former, users gain access to charts that track Bitcoin value in relation to different fiat currencies.

Apart from this, users can also track the daily transaction volume for this particular cryptocurrency. Although there are some investors who only worry about their own coins, a significant number of Bitcoin owners actually find value in information such as trade volumes.

This is because the number of actively used coins can have an impact not only on prices but supply and demand. With this information on hand, you can make better deals and smarter decisions when it comes to the cryptocurrencies that you own and are trading.

Just like other trackers online, you can customize Coinbase to your liking. This means that you can set time ranges for your graphs. If there is a downside, it is that users will not know where the tracker gets its information from, as the provider does not disclose such information.

3. CoinDesk

CoinDesk is another excellent tracker to give a go. What sets it apart from other cryptocurrency trackers is its provision of its own BPI or Bitcoin Price Index. This index run a comparative analysis of three major Bitcoin exchanges namely BTC-e, Bitfinex, and Bitstamp.

Using the information it gathers, users are provided with a graphical display that includes the BPI plus individual prices from these three exchanges. Apart from these, the tracker also gives you side-by-side access to Mt. Gox historical data.

Users do not only gain access to real-time rates but also get to decide if they want opening and closing prices to be displayed together with daily highs and lows. If you want to closely monitor rates then this may be an ideal tracker to use.

There are other excellent trackers available in the Internet but these three are the best to start with. Over time, and as you try other trackers out, you will be better calibrated when deciding on which one suits your needs the most.

CHAPTER 9

THE FUTURE OF CRYPTOCURRENCIES

When the concept of Bitcoins first came to light, it was ridiculed by many and supported by a few. These days, the market for Bitcoins and other cryptocurrencies are rapidly growing at exponential rates that can no longer be ignored. In line with the evolution of money, many are expecting cryptocurrencies to garner a larger share of the monetary pie.

The Cryptocurrency Environment

Cryptocurrencies are more complex that what people may have been thinking and it is actually this complexity that makes it an able player in the growth of the financial society. But of course, there are challenges that can be expected if cryptocurrencies are expected to continue on its path of growth starting with enhancing the trading background.

Basically, cryptocurrencies are digital monetary assets traded over digital exchanges and stored in cyberspace wallets. This is why it is important to have enough authorization, encryption, and security protocols in place if these were to be transformed into everyday financial assets.

It is suggested that the market and exchanges will be more regulated than it currently is. There is also the suggestion to reduce anonymity in exchange for security. For example, instead of anonymous trades, it may be better for transactions to be recorded on a universal log, a public record with multiple copies that enable tracking, monitoring, and updating. For one, this can eliminate problems with fraud wherein the same coins are used for multiple purchases.

This log should then be encrypted so that information is saved and backed up with every update. This means that even if the details can be changed with every new transaction, copies of the previous entries will still be available for backtracking. Think of it as freezing all previous entries with every update, making it easy for regulators to see what changes have been made at specific time periods and if there is any fraudulent activity that needs to be addressed.

As new entries are made, new backups or blocks as they are called should be created as well. It is with this concept that technologies like blockchains come to light. So basically, a blockchain is a digital chain of blocks or backups marking various cryptocurrency transactions at every conceivable moment possible. It is important to have continuous improvements in blockchain technology if cryptocurrencies are wished to become primary monetary solutions in the years to come.

Online Neutrality

Online neutrality is extremely important in conversations relating to cryptocurrencies. In general, what you have here is something that aims to protect not only content creators but businesses as well. Protection comes in the form of active regulation for large-scale corporations not to mention Internet service providers that are trying to monopolizing the trade.

Without this regulation in place, it is completely legal for the latter agencies to disrupt service not to mention enforce censorship as they see fit. And all of this can be done without these agencies ever being held liable for their actions leaving consumers to suffer a tremendous expense.

In the case of cryptocurrencies, the enforcement of regulations with regard to online neutrality can be attributed to its exponential growth. With proper measures in place, people are seeing cryptocurrencies as a worthwhile and very secure investment option. Desirable price increases for coins as well as growing international support are the results of proper regulation.

People and governments have become tolerant of these digital assets while global markets welcomed the entry of new offerings for active trading. As a result, the cryptocurrency market became more established, credible, and of course, profitable. Should there be no active online neutrality regulation, it is possible for the cryptocurrency market to enter a bubble which can then be popped on a whim by monopolistic corporations.

The thing about cryptocurrencies is that even if they are promising additions to the financial and technological spaces, there still remain a conservative few that consider them to be abominations or disruptions to the system. A number of Internet service providers share this sentiment and would be pleased to send cryptocurrencies into oblivion.

This is because with the continuous expansion of potential applications for cryptocurrencies, they are seen as potential threats to the technological services that Internet service providers offer. And if cryptocurrencies garner enough support, it may be possible for them to overtake these companies and send them into a complete financial downfall. So before this can happen, they are actively working to eliminate cryptocurrencies for good.

Some ways by which these companies are sabotaging cryptocurrencies in the absence of adequate neutrality laws is by reducing broadband speeds for related sites like blockchains and exchanges. In doing so, they slow down transaction speeds in the hopes of influencing patrons to up and go. Blockchains and exchanges are not that susceptible to manual intervention but they still rely on broadband connections to operate.

And although the absence of online neutrality is not the only factor that can bring cryptocurrencies down, it remains to be a primary concern in their evolution. This is why it is important for such a concern to be made public early on as it will help educate people in the hopes of saving the reputation of cryptocurrencies for the years to come.

Cryptocurrency Evolution

It was in 2009 when people became aware of cryptocurrencies thanks to the emergence of Bitcoin. It has remained one of the most popular digital currencies available today, but with the rapid growth of the concept came about other variations that are slowly drowning out Bitcoins.

Currently, there are close to two thousand different cryptocurrencies that people can invest in. Out of these options, there is about a fourth being actively traded in different exchanges. Based on the ongoing research into the market, these cryptocurrencies alone are worth over $50 billion.

And unlike other monetary assets that fluctuate not only in price but popularity, cryptocurrencies have remained strong in financial markets garnering and maintaining significant shares over time. And based on current market activities, there are no signs of this rapid growth ever slowing down in the near future. This just shows how well people have embraced cryptocurrencies as potential complements or alternatives to paper money.

In line with the specific Bitcoin market, it continues to perform at an above-average level. But there are other currencies like Ether that are quickly catching up and can be expected to overthrow Bitcoin in the near future; the reason being that new currency releases are addressing the issues investors are facing when it comes to their predecessors.

Aside from Bitcoin, other cryptocurrencies that you should be watching out for include Ether, Monero, Litecoin, and Ripple. Currently, their market shares total in at 20% of the active trading segment. In about a decade, it has been projected that Bitcoin's market share will dwindle by as much as 50% in support for these alternatives. A potential issue that can be attributed to this is Bitcoin's increasing volatility.

But this goes without saying that there is still a bright future that can be expected for Bitcoins, especially the different technologies that surround it, blockchains included. For as long as there is always an active effort in expanding the application of cryptocurrencies, it can be expected that these digital assets will continue reaching new heights as time progresses.

There are also plenty of individuals who are positively hoping that more financial instruments will be linked with cryptocurrencies in one way or another. When this happens, more people will be more than willing to invest in the digital currency market and its application will extend far beyond just being an alternative for direct payment.

And as Ethereum brought about the concept of smart contracts, it is expected that these continue on with other cryptocurrencies further expanding the usability of these online coins. If you have not heard of smart contracts, what you have here are digital protocols that serve the purpose of executing contract terms. This works by eliminating the need for intermediaries thereby enhancing the efficiency of contractual dealings or transactions.

And finally, there is the expectation that cryptocurrencies will be better able to address both the issues of anonymity and privacy. Currently, Zcash is offering a fully anonymous form of digital currency where transactions are not named nor are there any amounts recorded on blockchains. As for the latter, it requires an investment of time and technology to ensure that the cryptocurrency exchange will not lead to fraudulent transactions.

But all in all, there are very high hopes for cryptocurrencies and more than enough support to see them through. All people have to do is wait and see where this revolutionary technology takes them and hopefully that is towards the best path possible for financial evolution.

CONCLUSION

Modern-day technology continues to improve day in and day out. And apart from the development of various devices, we too are in an age where digital currencies are created.

Cryptocurrencies are digital assets that hold value. They can be used to make purchases online and offline. They can also be held as investments. Functioning closely like traditional stocks, these are great financial tech instruments for those who want to earn a passive income on the side.

There are different elements though that you need to familiarize yourself with before investing in these cryptocurrencies. Doing your research and studying up on the different coin types, exchanges, wallets, and components will ensure that your transactions run safely.

After reading this book, I hope that you've gained ample knowledge about cryptocurrencies to be able to find enough confidence to get started. Just make sure that you do not act hastily as you are still participating in a monetary market.

In this case, it is important that you take your time, practice, and of course, have fun.

The next step is to find some coins to buy, an exchange to try, and a wallet to keep them well secured. Good luck!

Finally, if you enjoyed this book, please consider leaving a review at the platform. Reviews are one of the easiest ways to support the work of independent authors.